The Moors of Cornwall

Michael Williams

BOSSINEY BOOKS

First published in 1986
by Bossiney Books
St Teath, Bodmin, Cornwall.
Printed and bound in Great Britain by
A. Wheaton & Co. Ltd, Exeter.

ISBN 0 948158 11 5

Plate Acknowledgments

Cover photograph by Ray Bishop
Marylou North: pages 5, 6, 9, 47-51, 54-58, 64-70, 73 right,
75-80, 82, 84-88, 92, back cover upper
Ray Bishop: pages 7, 8, 13, 14, 17, 18, 21-25, 30-35
37-45, 71, 72, 73 left, back cover lower
Felicity Young: pages 11, 19, 20, 29, 53, 56, 60, 62, 89, 90
Royal Institution of Cornwall: pages 16, 27, 28, 81
Woolf-Greenham Collection: pages 36, 55
George Ellis: page 83

ABOUT THE AUTHOR – AND THE BOOK

A Cornishman, Michael Williams started full-time publishing in 1975. With his wife Sonia, he runs Bossiney Books from a cottage and converted barn in North Cornwall – they are literally cottage publishers, specializing in Westcountry subjects by Westcountry authors. For ten years they ran the Bossiney House Hotel, just outside Tintagel – hence the name Bossiney Books.

Outside publishing and writing, Michael Williams is a keen cricket enthusiast. He is President of the Cornish Crusaders Cricket Club and a member of the Cornwall and Gloucestershire County Clubs. He is also a member of the RSPCA, and has actively worked for reform in laws relating to animal welfare. In 1984 he was elected to the Ghost Club and remains convinced Cornwall is the most haunted area in Great Britain.

In *The Moors of Cornwall*, Michael Williams travels first across the Moors of Penwith, then on to the Goss Moor, and finally over Bodmin Moor. 'These areas,' he says, 'may retain deep secrets like some of the pools that lie across the landscape, but they have a revitalizing quality too.' Nearly all the photographs and drawings have been especially commissioned for the book. 'No-one can ever say he or she really knows the Moors,' he reflects, 'for the Moors give us much, but only so much. You cannot "do" the Moors of Cornwall – not even in a lifetime – because they are a renewing experience – there are *always* revelations in store.'

THE MOORS OF CORNWALL

The Moors of Cornwall have a special magic.

They may be smaller than Dartmoor but they still have strange mystery and power.

It was the painter and writer Charles Simpson who first introduced me to the magic of our moors. Back in the 1920s he had provided the illustrations for a book called *Unknown Cornwall* written by C. E. Vulliamy.

'Less vast, less lofty than the moors of Devon,' wrote Vulliamy more than half a century ago, 'but infinitely more mysterious, more varied in form and mood, the Cornish moors have a penetrating charm which is peculiar to themselves. In all aspects they have a strange, almost a menacing beauty; something that eludes worldly striving; mutable yet eternal, transient as the shadow of a cloud, yet steadfast as the granite on their brows…'

Incredibly, thankfully, today our Moors of Cornwall retain the power and magnetism which drew Charles Simpson and kindred spirits to them.

As I explore them nowadays, I try and picture Charles travelling across them on painting expeditions – with his motor-cycle and sidecar – I think too of the year 1914 when a fisherman, out on Bodmin Moor, encountered a farmer quite unaware of the fact that we had been at war with Germany for more than two months!

On these journeys across the Moors of Cornwall, we have tried to evoke their individual spirit – I say 'we' because the illustrators on this expedition are very much co-authors.

Time, money and space have compelled us to be selective. A comprehensive volume on our Cornish Moors would need a thousand pages – and could still be incomplete.

We have divided them into three groups. First, the Moors of Penwith, then the Goss Moor, and finally Bodmin Moor.

Penwith is a perfect place for a beginning. Out on the Moors of Penwith, you somehow feel close to the beginning of things – even if Land's End and the Lost Land of Lyonesse are not far away. There is an enigmatic something on these last and first Moors of Britain. You *know* you're in the last quarter of the twentieth century, yet you *feel* on the edge of the prehistoric, memories and memorials of other races surround you, almost haunting.

Right: **King Arthur's Hall on Bodmin Moor. 'I cannot walk across the bleached grasses … and not feel related to earlier events.'**

Felicity Young at work by Charlotte Dymond's monument below Rough Tor.

The impact of moorland on a solitary traveller can be dramatic.

After a conversation with Charles Simpson, I resolved, one Saturday morning, to travel out from Penzance to climb up Carn Galva. Its serrated crest had a beckoning quality that grey November morning, and when I struggled to the top I found not only some of the greatest views in all West Cornwall but that it was the loneliest place in the world, frighteningly so, yet the majesty of the landscape conquered fear.

That was nearly thirty years ago. Then I didn't have the wit to know that when we *become part* of this lonely Penwith terrain various things happen to us. It's not only a question of going back in time – we certainly do that – but in a curious way pretence is

broken down and we begin to see our *real* selves. Out there that very still day, when the wind slept, the silence was something positive, eloquent in fact. Out there, too, I felt closer to God than in any ornate church.

The Moors of Penwith have invariably triggered some very fine painting.

Margo Maeckelberge of Penzance is one of our best known native painters. She also has a cottage and studio at Carne, high above Zennor. Carne, with its huge horizons and large expanses of moor, sky and sea has been the starting point of many of her paintings. D. H. Lawrence, who once lived at Zennor, called it 'a most beautiful place... high shaggy moor hills, a big sweep of lovely sea beyond...'

I asked Margo about Penwith's attraction for painters.

'The crystal-clear light is the explanation,' she said. 'When I've painted abroad and not found matching brilliance in the light, I've been disappointed and not satisfied as a painter. Today driving to St Ives and back over the moors, the strong light brought out all the vibrant form and colouring. It's this quality which has attracted painters over the years. Of course, the atmosphere's very stimulating too, but it's this brilliant light that gives everything a new meaning.

'Personally, too, I've always been haunted by the Atlantis legends, and my Atlanta series of paintings are the direct result of this haunting. Atlanta was the daughter of the king of Atlantis and when that terrible tidal wave engulfed the kingdom, Atlanta tried to escape and the Gods, seeing her attempts to escape

A broom flowers on the banks of the young Fal on the Goss Moor.

on the back of a dolphin, pitied her and turned her into part of this Celtic landscape of ours.

'So I see her everywhere, I see her in the rocks, in thrusting headlands, on the cliffs. I see a reclining nude and I see some rock formation and they're both Atlanta. You can't say I had an Atlanta period because it keeps coming back. The female is the land and the sea is the male. There's this constant embrace between the sea and the cliffs.'

Painters have a particular talent for opening our eyes, and I was especially lucky to meet Charles Simpson while still in my twenties. Despite a generation gap, he was a considerable influence. Thanks to Charles, I found myself walking across Hannibal's Carn – a new world after the coastline. Now I began to detect shade and subtlety in the Penwith landscape, the bracken for example, changing from the green of summer to the 'swarthy smouldering red of autumn'.

'Tracing the history of these relics,' he once put it, 'is like reading a book whose pages grow blurred and confused as the plot unfolds.' And relics meant anything from an ivy-coated cottage with crumbling masonry to some famous ancient monument.

These Moors, sprawling so close to the sea, intensify the doubt as to whether there can be such a thing as total myth. As we travel across these acres we shall be encountering various legends, and, more than once, we shall wonder whether there can truly be smoke without any fire.

Our Moors, like Dartmoor and Exmoor upalong, have been the breeding ground of some weird and wonderful tales. Maybe fellow Bossiney author Sally

Jones got close to the heart of the matter when she opened her *Legends of Cornwall* with this question: 'What is legend but gossip grown old?'

We need such territory, but we need to approach such places with humility. Provided we come with that humble spirit, then the Moor will speak, recharging us. These areas may retain deep secrets like some of the pools that lie across the landscape, but they have a revitalizing quality too.

Sally thoughtfully added: 'Certainly the legends of Cornwall make a fascinating patchwork of gossip, scandal and anecdote. Some deal with real people, historical figures whose real life stories have been embellished with a generous helping of exaggeration and the Supernatural.'

The Moors, too, have a haunted – haunting – atmosphere, genuinely so. Before we go any further on our journey, I should explain that I believe the case for ghosts is overwhelming.

Sculptor Sven Berlin, who once lived and worked in St Ives, told me: 'As far as I am concerned one is always living on the edge of two worlds, particularly in Cornwall, where divisions seem to be thinner and basic forces stronger.' Sven Berlin went on to remind me: 'De la Mare said he did not feel safe again until he had crossed the Tamar – going east,' and the poet never came back.

I cannot walk across the bleached grasses of a Cornish Moor, wind in my face, and not feel related to earlier events. Many of us, natives, live in the past as well as the present, and in these remoter regions that realisation is often strongest.

A Cornish Moor can work on us in a curious individual way. Some years ago Denys Val Baker related an interesting story, when he was dining with us at Bossiney. He used the cottage of a friend in Penwith, as the setting for a story. 'I attempted to capture the elemental side of life in Cornwall,' Denys explained. He was very attracted by the hills and moorland, and in this story he coupled the landscape to the Bohemian lifestyle of artists and writers, bringing the tale to a climax with a mock observation of ancient Druidic sacrifices. 'In my story there was a death and I was shaken to find out later that in real life there was a similar case of someone going to spend a night there only to be found dead next morning!' Denys called it 'a sort of pre-vision'. Frankly I am convinced these ancient moorland areas can and do work on us in quite remarkable fashion.

Some words of warning then before we begin our exploration. Only some people will appreciate the Moors. Others, like De la Mare, will flee. Vulliamy told Charles Simpson, when he wandered the Moors, he wanted no 'prattling graduate or young woman at his elbow'. That may be an extreme view, but many, who truly savour the moorlands, would say walking alone is a supreme experience. At least avoid the herd and explore only with kindred spirits.

No-one can ever say he or she really *knows* the Moors, for the Moors may give us much – but only so much. You cannot 'do' the Moors of Cornwall – not even in a lifetime – because they are a renewing experience – there are *always* revelations in store.

Rough Tor: 'Less vast, less lofty than the moors of Devon, but infinitely more mysterious ...'

10

11

MOORS OF PENWITH

I begin with the Moors of Penwith because these, the most westerly Moors of Cornwall, first introduced me to the energy and beauty of moorland scenery.

They were, in a sense, on the doorstep – that simple fact and the influence of Charles Simpson brought me out on to them.

Until around my mid-twenties I had stuck to the coastline – like many of the visitors. Interestingly, too, I have found very few early photographs of the Moors. Even talented perceptive photographers, like Herbert Hughes, clung to the edge of the sea – seemingly seduced by the cliffs and the coves, the harbours and the golden sands and those crimson sunsets over the Atlantic.

Discovering the Moors for me was a shattering experience. Thirty years ago, relatively few people explored them. Thousands flocked to St Ives and Newquay, Falmouth and other resorts – while the Moors remained largely deserted. Only now would I admit to being quite frightened by the loneliness of some of those early settings.

Today I find the same solitude energising. Maybe that is all part of the business of growing up – or coming to terms with the Moor.

Though Charles Simpson fired my imagination in this area – largely through our conversations and his writing – it was the then modern school of painters who sharpened my vision. It was something deeper and more important than discovering that a painting, like a poem or a piece of music, can enrich personal experience. Without coming face to face with sculpture, pottery and especially the paintings, I would have grown into a different poorer person. Oddly enough, it was *inside* the walls of the Penwith Gallery in St Ives that I *first* began to understand. The colours and the tones, the shapes and the rhythms of Penwith, I started seeing them for the first time, *there*.

Coming out on to the Moors – Hannibal's Carn was the first I explored – also made me feel very Cornish. I felt related to the place – more so than when I had walked across golden sands in earlier days. The Moors dented a romantic vision. Out here, where you cannot use a word like 'pretty' or 'nice', I was suddenly aware of the harder side of Cornish life – even the cruelty. The relics of a mining past may *look* romantic, but you then begin to understand that life

Right: **The Moors of Penwith first introduced me to the energy and beauty of moorland scenery.**

for the miner was tough, dangerous, precarious, capable of ruining a man. The mines were also capable of ruining men of wealth, the mine owners.

Peter Lanyon, the painter, often glided over this area of Penwith. His death, the result of a gliding accident at the age of 46, robbed Cornwall of one of her most famous sons.

He talked and wrote vividly and for 'an insider', a native Cornishman, he wrote with remarkable detachment, probably as he painted.

Here is something he contributed to the ill-fated *Cornish Review*: 'On carns of Zennor, Hannibal and Galva, where giants may have hurled their googlies in mild recreation, an outline of earthenwork makes evidence for a primitive brotherhood of man, of the great and small in life and death, wherein animal joy and terror found resolution in the protective care of monolith and fort. Hereabouts, perhaps, the sun set westwards shifting down the monolith to bury the light of primitive fire and rose again in the hearts of men from the east. The saints were in Cornwall.

'From Levant to Wicca, an easterly direction, chimneys are crowned by brick flourish, and the towers are lichen-covered castellated and pinnacled. They rise upward out of the horizontal ground, as if the thrust of stone had surfaced to the call of the native, given up its wealth to his endeavour, and had

Right: **Peter Lanyon, the painter, often glided over this area of Penwith.**

16

been revealed by manufacture as an expression of inner intent. Invention, leading to extension of native culture, made present in time a process of ancient development. The craft and skill and meaning of the native journey are outward and revealed at the land surface.'

Nearly all these Penwith photographs have been taken by Ray Bishop of Wadebridge. Cornish born and bred, Ray started serious professional photography in 1951, and has gone on providing a marvellous service for publishers of all types for more than three decades. It was Editor Brenda Duxbury, who introduced Ray to Bossiney, and in ten years of full-time publishing, he has created more images for us than any other photographer.

Ray has produced photographs for both local and national newspapers and magazines – on one famous occasion every photograph which appeared in *The Cornish Magazine* was his. In 1981 he scooped for Fleet Street the dramatic, tragic shooting of a Securicor guard outside a Wadebridge bank.

Out on these Cornish landscapes Ray understands subtleties, changes of mood. He is, in fact, a photographer for all seasons. In many Bossiney titles he has been essentially co-author, his images drifting across the pages beautifully, evocatively.

Left: **John Michell's inn at Madron, circa 1870. Moormen of Penwith would certainly have enjoyed some ale here.**

A miner's eye view from Ding Dong Mine. 'The relics of a mining past may look romantic, but ... life for the miner was tough ...'

Lanyon Quoit

A noble character in the Penwith landscape is Lanyon Quoit. It is a stone chamber-tomb, and you need little imagination to see it as a giant's table. A mighty flat capstone is supported by three pillars, all combining to produce one of the largest – and some say most perfect – quoits in the kingdom. If legend is to be believed then King Arthur himself dined here on the eve of his final battle, when wise old Merlin predicted that Arthur and his chieftains would gather here again, close to the road which leads to Madron, just before the end of the world.

Unfortunately Lanyon Quoit, as we see it today, is not in its original form. Apparently around the time of the Battle of Waterloo it fell during a violent storm, and it is thought the uprights were damaged. The old people said it was once high enough for a rider on horseback to pass underneath.

Different aspects of Lanyon Quoit. *Right:* **Felicity Young's drawing with gulls coming inland: omen of a storm they say.** *Above:* **Ray Bishop's photograph of the ancient 'table' with Ding Dong seen on the skyline.**

Men-an-Tol

The terrain around Morvah is some of the most powerful in all Cornwall. It inspired Sally Jones in her *Legends of Cornwall* to write: 'This part of Penwith is so heavy with history and legend that at times the farms and cottages of today seem dwarfed by their backcloth – a landscape where in times past mighty dramas human and Supernatural, were played out, whose echoes and traces now remain ''stamped on these lifeless things''.'

Our visit on this occasion was to specifically visit Men-an-Tol – sometimes known as the Crick Stone – the most celebrated holed stone in Cornwall.

Even today, Men-an-Tol is reputed to have healing powers. Mothers of sickly children still come here, dragging their children through the hole in the central stone, 'nine times against the sun', to cure them of scrofula and rickets – as mothers have done for many generations.

Janet and Colin Bord in their excellent book *Mysterious Britain* suggest that certain stones can hold powerful currents passing through the earth. Could not therefore the hole serve as a focus for this power which would pass into the body of the child or adult climbing through? This could account for the increased vitality some people claim to have experienced on climbing through the stone.

Left: **Men-an-Tol through the eyes of painter Felicity Young.**

Ruined Penwith cottage near Men-an-Tol.

21

Men-an-Tol Studio

Not far away, just off the main road, is the Men-an-Tol Studio and print workshop run by Ian Cooke. Originally the Bosullow Schoolhouse, built in 1882 to replace the earlier schoolroom, it served this scattered mining and farming community until 1899, when the failure of the local mines had reduced the population to such an extent that there were only nine children attending. The Board, despite protests, closed the school, 'a carpenter was engaged to board up the windows', and in 1918 the County Council sold it to a St Ives spinster for £50. Until Ian Cooke bought the building in 1980 it was used as a dwelling house.

Today it has taken on a new lifestyle, housing an exhibition of landscape prints, etchings, linoprints and woodcuts – all produced and printed on the spot by Ian Cooke working a Kimber hand-operated etching press.

Born in London in 1938 Ian Cooke, after National Service in the Far East, studied graphic design at the Kingston School of Art, and later set up and ran a

The Old Schoolhouse, Bosullow. In April 1882 land was bought for £15.12s. on which to build the school to accommodate 36 children. A mason's tender for £210 was accepted along with a carpenter's tender for £81.18s.6d.

Ian Cooke by his Kimber hand-operated etching press at Men-an-Tol Studio.

'one-man' letterpress and offset-litho printing business until 1971 when he sold up and moved down to West Cornwall. Here he began drawing, and making linoprints, receiving energy and inspiration from this dramatic Penwith landscape.

He has now renovated the old schoolhouse, and it is a delightful surprise to find an exhibition of work, here in the heart of the countryside, far removed from places like Newlyn and St Ives. Ian is also the author of a fascinating guide on the local monuments.

Men Scryfa

Authorship can be a splendid spur.

But for putting together this title, I may not have got to Men Scryfa – in Cornish it means the stone of writing. Though I had been to the Men-an-Tol before, I had somehow missed this granite pillar commemorating the death of a Celtic warrior of Roman birth.

It is, in fact, only a few minutes walk away from Men-an-Tol. Today it stands in the middle of a field, bearing the words RIALOBRANI CUNOVALI FILI – the last word is now below ground. The words are carved into the weatherbeaten northern face and mean 'Rialobran son of Cunoval'.

Ian Cooke, in his guide of the area, says an invader attacked the Glorious Prince, and seized his lands. The defeated royalty fled, but the Royal Raven resolved to regain his father's territory and a great battle took place on these moors where the stone stands.

Though the Prince was killed, presumably he won his battle. The presence of the monument here must mean that his father's lands were recaptured. It is said he was buried beneath the stone and the height of the stone was precisely his height. Some believe the stone is nine feet tall. Yet on the Sunday morning in July when I stood beside it, it seemed more like six feet – but who knows how many feet lie beneath the ground?

They also say the Prince's arms and treasures were buried with him. Greed proved too much for one local miner. Hungry for gold, he dug underneath the stone, causing the monument to fall, nearly crushing him in the process. Happily the stone was re-erected around 1824.

24

Author at Men Scryfa.

Zennor

Hereabouts there is a marvellous Cornish combination: the moors almost running down to the cliffs and the sea. It can be a magical experience in the evening.

'On a warm summer night the moonlight gleaming on the granite and the sea full of phosphorus are not to be forgotten,' wrote Sir John Betjeman in his *Cornwall*, a Shell Guide. 'All along the higher ground, as though they wanted to be away from the rough coast itself, early man built dwelling places, temples and tombs. They look like the work of a race of Giants.'

One especially fine example is Zennor Quoit. Invisible from the road, but less than a mile away as the Cornish Chough once flew, even in its ruined condition – vandalised by a Georgian farmer – Zennor Quoit remains a noble monument.

Someone has said in Penwith you find yourself walking among the early instalments of history. I certainly felt that as I came face to face with this battered dolmen. Belonging to the Megalithic Age – the great stone period – Zennor Quoit can only be vaguely dated; somewhere between 2000 and 1500 BC. Bodies of the dead were brought here.

Hereabouts too the landscape in a farming sense has a very distinctive quality. The hedges, enclosing the green fields, are made of enormous grey boulders. Sarah Foot has referred to them as 'Checker-board stone walled fields'. There's a substantial air too in the sense that some of the very old cottages and farm buildings are made of great blocks which must have taken a team of sturdy Cornishmen to lift into position.

Right: **A wayside chat at Zennor 1894: farm to the west of Churchtown.**

Right: **Zennor Quoit: Felicity Young working in this instance from an old photograph.**

Below: **The Giant's Stone at Zennor photographed in the year 1903 by that splendid photographer Herbert Hughes.**

29

Wayside Museum, Zennor

Right: **Looking east from the Museum gardens with Zennor Hill beyond. The roadsign is the last survivor showing the old title of 'Zennor Churchtown'.**

Not until around the beginning of the nineteenth century were roads made into Zennor. Pack animals and sledges rather than the conventional cart brought goods here. Consequently Zennor remained more remote than most villages, an isolation intensified by the shape of the land and the sea.

The visitor to Zennor today owes a considerable debt to Colonel 'Freddie' Hirst. One day in the 1930s, the Colonel, standing on Hayle Quay, studying a hillock of scrap-metal bound for Germany, noted how many strange tools and implements were being shipped away as mere 'scrap'. That experience triggered ideas, and before long he was searching among the old barns and mowhays of Penwith.

The result is The Wayside Museum, founded in 1935, covering aspects of life in and around Zennor

Left: **The kitchen at Wayside: hardly altered since the sixteenth century. The hearth is still fully functional with many original utensils and implements. Old folk who have tasted food cooked on a hearth say there is nothing to compare with it.**

31

from 3000 BC to our twentieth century. Run by caring resident curators Richard and Betty Williamson, this unique museum is well worth a visit. You can profitably spend an hour or two here or the greater part of the day. It is a peaceful place. The collection of implements and relics peculiar to this corner of Penwith are housed in the ground floor rooms of the old miller's house, in the old mill, several outbuildings and the garden. The kitchen, with its open hearth, is a gem, somehow enabling us to get a glimpse of a vanished way of Penwith life; while the mill, with original machinery and millstones, sharing the walls and roof with a blacksmith's shop all combine to take us back in time and mood. A visit here is more vital than any history book; for inside these walls we get the *feel* of how moorland folk, long ago, lived and worked.

The Wheelwright's Shop which is really a tribute to all craftsmen in wood. Wheelwrights, shipwrights, joiners, sawyers or coopers would all find familiar tools and accessories here. The hay wagon, built in 1922, is displayed with the tools that were used in its construction.

Left: Vehicles from the collection of tin mining relics at Wayside. Nearest the camera is a flat-topped 'dandy' used for carrying tools. Next is the famous side-loading tram and in the background a horse-drawn water wagon of about 1870. Water was sold to the miners at a rate of one penny per bucket – this may account for their preferring something stronger!

The Hooting Carn

'Carn Kenidjack or Carn Idzhek, is a place of terrors. It is known as the Hooting Carn. A mass of piled and shattered granite, capping the moorland about a mile and a half north-east of St Just, with a fantastic stony dishevelment – a clumsy, crazy and sinister outline. The fiends of hell, dark and monstrous figures, resort to this place, so they say, at night; and you may see the glimmer of a ghostly light about the rocks of the Carn and coming and going of black, massive forms. Over the heaths of Carnyorth and Truthwall, among the burial mounds and the circles and the ancient stones, a cloaked horseman on a lean and spectral horse rides in pursuit of the homeless dead.'

Those lurid words came from the pen of C. E. Vulliamy. More than sixty years on, the Hooting Carn remains a haunting, haunted corner of Penwith.

Moreover, there are genuine claims of phantom hoofbeats in the St Just area.

Ethel Waters, who lived at Chyoone Farm for many years, is quite convinced these hoofbeats are of a Supernatural nature. She first told me about her experiences when she lived at the farm. 'I hear them coming down the road. They stop outside here, and it always happens in stormy weather. I heard them first soon after we came here to live. I heard this clatter of hooves and the rumble of a carriage, or coach. A funny time to bring horses out I thought. It was late at night and the strange thing was I didn't hear them drive away. So, when it happened again, I checked up and went outside... nothing... no sign of horses or carriage or coach. But I definitely heard them come down the road. Certain of it. Funny thing is, I'm always alone when I hear them...'

Recently, I had another conversation with her on the subject – she now lives in St Just but remains convinced.

'How often did you hear them?' I asked.

'At least thirty times, and always in stormy weather,' she replied. 'At first, I didn't take much notice of the noises; judging by the hoofbeats, at least a couple of horses, I'd say. And I've mentioned it to people outside the family. "Oh rubbish!" they'd say. But it wasn't rubbish. We had an alsatian dog and when she heard the hooves she'd raise her hackles. That was proof enough for me... it wasn't dreaming or imagination. The dog heard them all right.'

Furthermore Ethel Waters has a definite theory about the whole business. 'They say the road outside the farmhouse was an old turnpike road, and perhaps there was a toll house there... after all, it was near the start of the road... and this road going down to Tregeseal could have been important. Down at the end it meets five other roads, and one of them is the

Right: **Craggy shapes on the Hooting Carn.**

coast road to St Ives. I'm only guessing about the toll house, but I'm not guessing about *hearing* the horses. I heard them too often for that...'

In the light of that kind of experience, cynicism shrinks and it is the Doubting Thomas who begins to look the charlatan.

Below Carn Kenidjack stands a real Penwith mystery: the Tregeseal Stone Circle.

It may not have the grandeur of the Hurlers up on Bodmin Moor, but these stones have a magic of their own. A while back, I walked there with two friends,

Peter and Enid Thomas, who live nearby at Truthwall. It was afternoon, and I had already had a long and not easy day of business, having set out from North Cornwall at seven o'clock that morning. Yet I came away from the circle renewed and refreshed. It was a tonic to be there.

Tom Lethbridge, that great seeker of the truth and master dowser, was convinced there are forms of energy which we do not begin to understand. I thought of him and his theories, that afternoon, as I came away from the circle at Tregeseal.

Above: **Looking down on St Just and the Atlantic from Carn Kenidjack.**

Left: **Tregeseal stone circle with Carn Kenidjack in the background.**

GOSS MOOR

As you stand by the source of the Fal on Goss Moor – it's little more than a gentle gurgle of water – you begin to appreciate the wonder of Nature. I say 'begin' because it is hard to fully comprehend that this tiny ribbon of water eventually turns into one of the great Cornish rivers.

Whenever Sonia and I take the car across the King Harry Ferry and we look at those huge tankers laid up on the broad waters of the Fal, I have to think back to this modest beginning on the Moor.

It can be no accident that some of the finest scenery in Cornwall is to be found by rivers – unashamed

Left: **Ponies on Goss Moor.** *Above:* **Fal 'lake' near Indian Queens, with the hilltop church at St Dennis on the horizon.**

moor man that I am, I readily admit this. The undeniable fact is rivers are among the most graceful things in all Nature. The country through which a river flows somehow gains in vitality and then, as a balance, there is the serenity which comes from quiet pools.

Here on the edge of Goss Moor is the china clay country. Of this mysterious terrain our great Cornishman and poet, Charles Causley, once wrote: 'This is the lunar and the lunatic landscape of the moon: a weird, white world, dusted over with the colour of sex, where workers are like walking wedding cakes.'

This, for me, will always be Jack Clemo country. Jack Clemo, despite great problems of sight and hearing, has emerged as one of Cornwall's outstanding writers and one of Britain's 'finest landscape poets'.

I interviewed him nearly a quarter of a century ago and asked him how the china clay country had shaped his thinking and his writing.

'The china clay country gave me exactly the kind of images I needed in presenting my ideas of religion and sex. It is too artificial to be of much value to those who want to develop a pagan philosophy. The constant blasting and excavating suggested to me the violent Christian attack on complacent natural processes, while the stiff white breasts and clay beds remind me of a rare kind of sexuality different from that of the farms and woods. The element of fantasy; the almost fairy-land effects of the weird shapes and the various lights after nightfall, were all so very potent in stirring and moulding my imagination.'

Right: **Another view of the Fal 'lake', and,** *left,* **the source of the River Fal on Goss Moor near Roche.**

Above: **Demelza Chapel built in 1871, with caretaker at the entrance and geese disappearing up the lane.**
Below: **Inside Demelza Chapel.**

Demelza

It must have been thirty years ago, when driving across the Goss Moor, somewhere between Indian Queens and Victoria that I first saw the sign to Demelza.

It had a magical ring – still has – and nearly twenty years later I met my first live Demelza: Demelza Val Baker, daughter of the Cornish author. Later too, I fell under the magical spell of the Welsh actress Angharad Rees who played Demelza in the brilliant BBC television series based on the Poldark novels.

And later still I had the luck to dine with the man who created this great Cornish saga, Winston Graham. We were being entertained by Kate and Dennis Hocking at Carlyon Bay, and midway through dinner I asked Winston Graham about Demelza and was intrigued to learn that he had 'discovered' her name on that very signpost on the Goss Moor.

Not until October 1983 did Sonia and I go down that narrow winding lane, which leads to the hamlet of Demelza. It was a place I had curiously avoided – afraid of being disappointed. It is no Cornish gem, but we loved it and on a sunny October afternoon that might have been borrowed from late summer, the only traffic we encountered were five riders on horseback.

The little chapel there, built in 1871, now holds a service just once a month. If you forget the TV aerials and the telephone cables, this is inland Cornwall as our grandparents knew it: hamlets, cottages and isolated farms. Long may Demelza stay that way.

Greystones

There are relatively few Moorland hotels in Cornwall. But if you are thinking of staying somewhere near a Moor and fairly central for Cornwall as a whole, I have a recommendation.

Greystones is a renovated farmhouse on the main A30 between Bodmin Moor and Goss Moor. Run by the resident proprietors Bet and Bill Mansell, Greystones provides spacious comfortable accommodation with genuine old furniture and brass beds. Several of the bedrooms are en-suite – and the visitors book is punctuated with generous comments. Moreover Bet Mansell has a wonderful way with animals. They have horses available for experienced riders – and she positively delights in providing 'hotel accommodation' for cats whose owners are away on holiday or on business. Her four-footed friends receive five-start treatment: good food, quarters – above all, there is love and concern for every individual cat.

Roche Rock

One of the great landmarks of Cornwall stands on the edge of the Goss Moor: Roche Rock.

This beautiful old ruin is rich in legend. The story goes that when Tristan wanted to bring about a reconciliation between Iseult and King Mark, he asked Ogrin the hermit to act as a kind of go-between.

Cornwall, over the years, has given sanctuary to many hermits, and this is surely one of the loveliest hermitages to be found anywhere. Ditmas in his book on the Tristan story suggested that Beroul might have been thinking of the hermitage at Roche Rock.

Anyway the ruins are still here, clinging stubbornly to the rock – rather like a John Piper painting – a hundred feet high crowning a granite crag, a tower with the hermit's cell below and chapel above, dating from the fifteenth century.

Another legend links the hermitage with Dozmary Pool, and that Cornish rogue Jan Tregeagle. The unjust steward was charged for his various misdeeds and subsequently sentenced to bail out Dozmary with a leaky limpet-shell. Tregeagle, tortured by the impossibility of his task, fled to Roche Rock, where hammering and howling on the door of the chapel, he begged forgiveness and admission.

Children of earlier generations were told storm noises were really Tregeagle and his Hell Hounds out hunting. Hence the old Cornish expression: 'Howling like a Tregeagle'.

Two different angles of Roche Rock with, *above,*
Roche playing cricket below the famous rock.

BODMIN MOOR

Bodmin Moor, the best known of our Cornish Moors, stretches twelve miles north to south and eleven miles east to west – small, of course, when you think of Dartmoor spreading itself over 365 square miles.

But it has wonderful variety: changes in landscape and mood, an area steeped in history and folklore. Here the twentieth century and distant past merge into a curious tapestry – in places it is difficult to disentangle past from present or fact from fiction.

Here is how E. V. Thompson described this aura of the past in his *100 Years on Bodmin Moor*:

'If you climb Stowe's Hill and look across Witheybrook Marsh to Langstone Downs on a winter's day, when the grass and fern of the Moor has died back, the outlines of the first moorland fields can be clearly seen. Turn around, and behind you is the loose-stone stockade of an Iron Age fort, unexplored by modern man. Beyond the fort, past the balancing rocks of the Cheesewring, and the depths and spoil heaps of the Cheesewring Quarry, are the Hurlers. These three stone circles are dated *circa* 1500 BC, their purpose lost in the mists of antiquity.

'All around these ancient artifacts are the ruined enginehouses – memorials of yet another age. On the adjoining hill is the twentieth-century mast that beams television pictures to the homes of Cornwall. It was here, almost 150 years ago, that a rich copper strike was made by a Cornish mine captain. On the same spot in August 1644, King Charles I, with Prince Maurice mustered his Royalist troops before riding off to score a notable victory over his Parliamentarian opponents. Standing in this one spot, a man is aware of being surrounded by the history of 3,500 years.'

In some parts of the Moor, a century ago can seem only like yesterday. In the remoter areas time appears to contract. In some of the wilder, more desolate places, I get a strange sense of conflict: pleasure and unease. Pleasure at the beauty and grandeur – you cannot use words like pretty or nice about the Moor – and yet still a certain unease because this landscape makes you feel strangely vulnerable.

Beautiful deception surrounds you: tufts of grass, reedy stems – enchanting to the eye – but you need to use your eyes for other reasons. A foot in the wrong place, the ground begins to sag, the realisation of oozing water, and panic is not far away.

The tors which crown this beautiful but wicked

Right: **The two highest points in Cornwall –
Brown Willy and Rough Tor.**

Moorland travel 1985 – at St Breward.

country defy generalisation. Some are smooth and sleek like downlands; others are peaked with granite: crowns that give them a sinister air. On top of the higher tors the air is that of mountains: cold and pure.

Marylou North is a fine young photographer who knows Dartmoor well. She has lived for several years near Chagford. Bodmin Moor, on the other hand, was practically an unknown kingdom for her. This is why

I commissioned her to do most of the Bodmin Moor photographs.

I asked Marylou for first impressions.

'Bodmin is superficially the same as Dartmoor,' she said, 'Dartmoor on a smaller scale, in that you have the same elements... granite, open heath, tors, grazing stock and few trees. But their characters are quite different.

Right: **Bolventor Church – at time of publication under threat of closure.**

48

'Dartmoor is much more a separate entity whereas Bodmin tends to merge into the surrounding countryside. Its edges are not so easily defined. Possibly because it's lower you don't ascend onto the Moor in the same way as Dartmoor. Also on Dartmoor the geology has produced dramatic valleys on the edge of the Moor.

'But for the photographer you have this lovely light on Bodmin, thrown up on north and south sides from the sea... a light that you only get on the western side of Dartmoor.'

She found Dozmary 'a strange evocative place'.

Marylou's photographs – to me – have caught the essential qualities of Bodmin Moor. It was, I think, the great David Bailey who said, 'Black and white pictures are more difficult to do, but they leave more to the imagination. It is the difference between a newsreel and a still picture: one explains everything, the other raises questions.'

Looking at her moorland pictures made me understand what Mr Bailey was saying – and meaning.

Jamaica Inn

The most famous moorland inn of Cornwall and arguably in the British Isles is Jamaica Inn, a slated Georgian building, standing high in the landscape at Bolventor.

Once a Temperance House, later a club and now, thanks to the brilliant story-telling of Dame Daphne du Maurier, a Cornish landmark. In our hotel days, we encountered American visitors who had come to Cornwall to see just three things: King Arthur's Castle at Tintagel, Land's End, and Jamaica Inn.

Dame Daphne's novel *Jamaica Inn* remains one of my favourite Cornish books. A tale of dark events along the Cornish coastline culminating here, featuring a memorable Cornish heroine Mary Yellan, it is Daphne du Maurier at her most beguiling.

Why Jamaica Inn?

One theory is that the original house was built by a Jamaican settler; another that the name grew naturally out of Jamaica: the home of rum.

And not all the strange stories relating to Jamaica Inn are fiction. In the bar, many years ago, a stranger was enjoying a tankard of ale – a tankard he never finished – for he was called outside, and disappeared into the night. Next day they found his body out on the Moor, but the identity of his murderer was never discovered: an almost perfect crime in fact.

Peter Underwood, the President of the Ghost Club, in his *Ghosts of Cornwall*, included this eerie tale and brought to light some interesting facts. 'More than one landlord has heard ghostly footsteps tramping

Jamaica Inn, at Bolventor, arguably the most famous moorland inn in Britain.

along the passage to the bar – are they those of the murdered man returning to finish his drink?

'Some years ago there was a great deal of correspondence in *Country Life* about a strange man who was often seen by many people sitting on the wall outside the inn; he never spoke or moved and his description seemed, from everyone's account, to have been so similar to that of the murdered stranger that it was thought that he must be the dead man's ghost.'

Right: **The Cheesewring stands on a famous ley line, beginning at St Michael's Mount, travelling through to this spot on Bodmin Moor, on to St Michael's Church at Brentor, up to Somerset to Burrow Mump and Glastonbury …**

The Cheesewring

On the eastern side of the Moor stands one of the great curiosities of Cornwall: the Cheesewring. Your immediate reaction is that it *must* be man-made – the stones balance so beautifully – but general belief is it's a natural formation. Henry Moore or Barbara Hepworth produced nothing more beautiful, more dramatic.

Try and come here on a crystal-clear day and you will be richly rewarded. From these grey-blue stones whole chunks of both Cornwall and Devon are visible: the English Channel to the south and the Atlantic to the north. Eastward sprawls Dartmoor and if you are really lucky Exmoor too can be seen.

From such a pinnacle you get a definite feel of the Moor: the grey granite scattered across the brown and the greens of the landscape.

Daniel Gumb's Hut

Below the Cheesewring are the remains of Daniel Gumb's hut, one of the strangest, off-beat homes in all Cornwall.

Gumb, a stonecutter from Linkinhorne, was one of the most eccentric Moorland characters of all. At an early age he mastered the principles of algebra and Euclid. His real love, however, was the study of the skies at night and he became an authority on astrology.

This corner of the Moor is a wild place today. It must have been even wilder, more wicked in the 1700s when Daniel built his home of moorstones, with granite slabs for beds and chairs. He lived through three marriages here, paying neither rent nor tax.

He first married Joan – maiden name unknown – in

1732; Thomasine Roberts in 1735; and his third and last wife Florence Brockinshaw in 1743, by whom he had a large family. A curious mixture of a man: he was God-fearing yet he attended neither church nor chapel. He christened all the children himself on the ancient stone 'altars' of the Moor. Daniel Gumb spent hours wandering this moorland landscape, books in hand, or chipping away his distinctive geometrical designs on the grey rocks – some of which can be seen today – and at night he studied the wide dark skies above Caradon.

For all his eccentricity and the remoteness of his home, he had a sense of humour. There is evidence of it on a tombstone in St Melor's Churchyard at Linkinhorne, dated 1742. It seems there was disagreement between church dignitaries and the relations of two who had died as to whether the deceased should be buried inside or outside the church. Gumb carved the following words on one of the tombstones:

> Here we lye, without the wall,
> T'was full within, they made a brawl,
> Here we lye, no rent to pay,
> And yet we lye so warm as they.

More than once I have stood in front of the ruins of Gumb's hut and tried to picture it in his time – he died in 1776, leaving apparently no worldly wealth, only a diary describing his passion for the stars.

The ruins now lie roughly one hundred metres from their original site, and to get an idea of how the place really looked we have to go to the writings of John Harris. He came to this desolate spot a century and a half after the Gumbs had left and this is how he described it:

'... the entrance was rather low and narrow; the floor was full thirty feet long by ten or twelve feet wide, composed of sandy loam inclining towards one door, opposite which was a rude chimney. On the right hand side about three feet high was a bench of rock running nearly the whole length from three to four feet wide, along which ran a stout fir pole. This formed the sleeping place. On the left two other benches stood, one lower than the other, serving for sitting and table.'

Daniel Gumb's cave.

Left: **A mining relic near Minions.**

The Hurlers

On the edge of the Moor, hard by the village of Minions, stands The Hurlers, another mysterious stone circle or, more precisely, three rings of stone. They have – for me – a strangely alluring quality. I find it virtually impossible to come to Minions and not be drawn to them. They somehow give the impression that they have been placed with scientific precision. Yet nobody knows *why* they stand here.

Minions is one of my favourite areas of all Cornwall. Times were when this was boom mining country. A few men made fortunes, but at an awful human price. Today the skeletons of the old engine houses give the landscape a nostalgic air; give it a certain sadness too – as if they were headstones in a cemetery which, in a way, they are.

56

Kilmar Tor and Lady Vyvyan

On more than one occasion I had the luck to discuss the business of writing about Cornwall with Lady Clara Vyvyan, our greatest native travel writer, then living at Trelowarren.

Nobody has written of Cornwall or the Cornish atmosphere with greater skill and sensitivity. Curiously, though, she confessed she often felt quite inadequate.

In *Cornish Silhouettes*, first published in 1924, she asked: '... who am I, presumptuous atom, trying to imprison the spirit of Cornwall in human words?' She went on to liken it to 'trying to chain the swallow, or build a castle with reflections, or fetter sunshine in a cage'.

Of the wild beauty of Cornwall, Lady Vyvyan once wrote wisely: 'I know that it is not captured and yet it is everywhere. It is very close, yet inaccessible as the stars. It is old and immeasurable, mysterious as the Dolmens and Menhirs outlined against the western sky, yet vital as the opening bud or the dawning sun. It has a myriad changing forms, but it is one and unchangeable...'

I thought of her words when I walked across Twelve Men's Moor in the direction of Kilmar Tor. One of the most majestic tors, it is an awe-inspiring sight. Words convey next to nothing. The traveller simply must go there and experience for himself or herself.

It can be a renewing, recharging experience.

Left: **Kilmar Tor on the skyline.**

60

Trethevy Quoit

Between Minions and St Cleer stands another majestic Cornish personality: Trethevy Quoit – sometimes known as Arthur's Quoit. A monument, probably to some ancient dynasty of chieftains, it dates from the Megalithic Age, 2000-1500 before the birth of Christ. Originally covered in earth to form a burial mound, Trethevy and Zennor are the only surviving quoits in Cornwall with a second chamber.

The athletic Sally Jones on her legendary journey crawled through a tiny aperture in the stone. I didn't follow in Sally's footsteps but asked her why she thought the tiny gap was there. There have been various theories: to allow the spirits of the dead to escape, to allow food to be placed inside as sustenance through eternity and, rather a contradiction to the first, to *prevent* the spirits of the dead from escaping.

Sally had a more down-to-earth explanation: 'To discourage grave robbers and, in later years, nosy people like me.'

King Doniert's Stone

There are places in Cornwall that stir your curiosity about people from the distant past. Down in Penwith, I wondered about the kind of man commemorated by that inscribed stone near the Men-an-Tol. Out on King Arthur's Downs I pondered about the great King, wondering how much belonged to fact and how much to myth – and whether he really hovered somewhere between the two.

Here by the side of the road, which links Redgate and Minions, I thought about King Doniert. The inscription in Latin on the stone tells us it was erected for 'the good of King Doniert's soul'. Some say he was the last King of Cornwall, but that distinction almost certainly belongs to King Ricatus who ruled in Cornwall in the tenth century, whereas Doniert died in 878. He drowned in the River Fowey. As I came away up the River Fowey valley, I stopped and looked at the growing river, and wondered how a King could have drowned in such an idyllic spot. It may have been a wilder place then, but you still wonder how and why.

Above: **The River Fowey in its early stages, travelling down the Fowey Valley below Bolventor.** *Right:* **Joan Bettinson with her Siamese cat, Blue.**

64

Joan Bettinson

Joan Bettinson is a 'wise woman' – some would call her a 'white witch'. She lives in an old miner's cottage in the village of Commonmoor on the edge of the Moor.

Once upon a time most Cornish villages boasted a charmer. But now they are a dying breed. Joan, who has successfully charmed warts and ringworm, is therefore in great demand today. Many people come down the winding narrow lane to Rosevale seeking a cure, and her mail comes from many countries.

A couple of years ago Sonia had an irritating stubborn rash – it just refused to go away despite various prescriptions – and, in desperation, I suggested she should phone Joan. Sonia and Joan, in fact, have never met. Yet, over the telephone, Joan was able to pinpoint the location of the rash, tell Sonia it had come from a cattle infection – and that it would go inside ten days.

Within seven days all traces of the rash had vanished from Sonia's leg – and there must be dozens and dozens of people who could testify as to Joan Bettinson's gifts.

Those gifts are not limited to healing either. Her intuition can be quite uncanny. She has the knack of picking up messages in the ether, and, though not a professional clairvoyante, she probes the future for relations and close friends by reading the tea leaves in tea cups.

Above all, she has a passion for Cornwall and all things Cornish, and for Bodmin Moor in particular. Joan is one of an old school, and I am proud to know her as a special moorland friend.

Here she is photographed at home with her Siamese cat Blue. They both have those blue eyes that I now instinctively look for in psychic folk – and Joan thinks the parallel true because she rates cats among the most psychic of the animal kingdom.

MCC–E

Jane Talbot-Smith

Jane Talbot-Smith lives and works in the lovely Fowey Valley.

The horse, for centuries, has been an integral part of the Moor, and she operates her one-woman business, Higher Harrowbridge Saddlery and Blisland Harness Makers at Higher Harrowbridge Farm, Bolventor.

Cornish-born, Cornish-educated, Jane Talbot-Smith is a highly talented all-rounder in leather. She specialises in light driving harness and top quality bridlework, but also makes rocking-horse saddles and bridles to order, braided belts, bellows, leather boxes and casework.

She went out of Cornwall to train in harness making – to Bridleways in Guildford, Surrey, where her tutor was Les Coaker, the man who made the side saddle the Queen uses at every Trooping of the Colour ceremony.

Watching her at work in her workshop one Saturday morning, reminded me of sculptors at work in St Ives, and Jane Talbot-Smith is not surprised by the association of ideas. 'Imagine the leather being like a piece of marble,' she says. 'The sculptor hits in the right place and has no trouble in shaping it... once you know *how* to work the leather, the work becomes relatively easy.'

Left: **Jane Talbot-Smith at work.**

Looking down on the Fowey from high ground above Lostwithiel.

Lionel Miskin

Though it was Charles Simpson, a painter of the old school, who first opened my eyes to the magic of moorland in Cornwall, it was another painter of another generation who made me understand the magical possibilities of Bodmin Moor in particular.

I only met Lionel Miskin once, but he made an enormous impression. We talked at Mevagissey by the sea, and this is how he saw the Moor.

'Bodmin Moor shares with the china clay country a certain starkness, an almost brutally present structure, suggesting petrified waves, crested at the tors, otherwise in deep, wide undulations. The deep recessions of ochre and golden grass in the winter and of green in spring only lightly cover a sculpture you know to be as black as iron or bronze, for ploughed or cut for peat, this blackness is laid bare in a geometric patchwork that is as dark as that of the clay country a few miles further west is white. Even the cattle on the Moor tend to be black.

'I've painted often, both on the high ground of the Moor and in the valley running down to Golitha Falls, and I've experienced a selfish pleasure... the place doesn't seem to interest other painters. I've yet to meet one at work there. An advantage hitherto unknown to landscape painters is the ability to paint from a car in really wild weather, to look out at the extraordinary shapes of clouds building up on the Moors for a powerful storm, to see the shapes of rock or hill appear and disappear in the clouds and watch the ignitions of the sun on their surfaces. Clouds are as fine as any subjects known to figurative art, a visibly transforming sculpture, and the light of wild, wet weather far excels that of acceptably fine sunshine and duster blue skies...'

Left: **Golitha Falls.**

Temple Church before reconstruction in 1883.
'An ash of considerable size,' according to E. H.
Sedding. Nest at the top presumably that of a
carrion crow.

Left: **Woods near Golitha Falls.**

Left: **Lilac tree blooms by the river below the 'Cathedral of the Moors' at Altarnun. Eyes automatically climb the tower of St Nonna. This 130 foot tower took more than a generation to construct.**

Right: Less photographed, less well known, is the Wesleyan Chapel at Altarnun. There were in fact close links between Methodists and Anglicans at Altarnun, separation came slowly, almost reluctantly. Samuel Hart, a one-time vicar here, said in 1821: 'There are no Papists in the parish, but many Wesleyan Methodists who for the most part frequent the Church.'

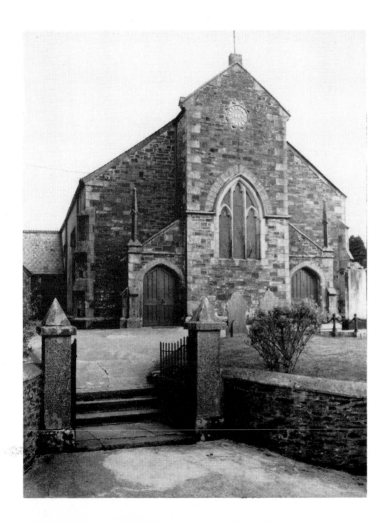

St Luke's – a moorland chapel, high on the shoulder of the Fowey Valley.

Dozmary Pool

Dozmary is a beautiful sheet of water, often silent, and sometimes sad.

'Nowhere else on earth,' wrote C. E. Vulliamy, 'are there landscapes more austerely beautiful, more wonderful in their changes of mood or colour, or more splendid in outline. The Pool in its placid moods, when it becomes a mirror reflecting the forms of moor and cloud, has a charm so powerful, yet so elusive, that it can only be conveyed to you in pictures: the limits of descriptive writing are soon exhausted.'

This is the pool into which Sir Bedevere was ordered to throw King Arthur's sword Excalibur.

Sarah Foot, who loves and understands the Cornish countryside, in her *Fowey – River and Town* has written: 'Its very beauty and surprising existence makes it understandably a place to give birth to wondrous stories. It is such a surprise to find, a mile in circumference, so high up, it does not seem to be fed by streams, stretched out like an enormous sparkling jewel in the midst of such wilderness. Like a moorland oasis.'

Sir John Betjeman once referred to 'a brooding melancholy, especially at evening' over Dozmary. I have heard too of Spiritualists who have come here to get in touch 'with the other side'. There *is* something unearthly about Dozmary. Excalibur may not be lying out there, but you get a feeling...

Left: **Dozmary Pool – a beautiful sheet of water.**

'Brooding melancholy' over Dozmary.

Right: **Ponies on King Arthur's Downs.**

Arthur on Bodmin Moor

At this point on our journey across Bodmin Moor, we find ourselves again on the Arthurian trail.

Arthur is a mystery. He has, in fact, grown into an international Agatha Christie theme – a detective operation turning scholar and archaeologist alike into Sherlock Holmes in an attempt to identify him.

Time was when I thought of Arthur as purely a legendary figure. Then I inclined to the view that there was *an* Arthur – not the courtly figure in shimmering armour on a charger, the picture in so many imaginations – but more the guerilla warfare fighter, like Tito in the last war.

Recently I have met members of a psycho-expansion group run by Barney Camfield of Plymouth, a Natural Healing Therapist and Unitarian Minister. They claim not only to have lived in Arthurian times, but some of them say they *were* Arthurian characters. The most extraordinary claim is that one, in fact, was King Arthur himself.

An Aquarian subject, a Westcountry housewife with brown eyes, I have interviewed her twice, both times under regression, and at length, an in-depth interview which appeared in *Strange Somerset Stories*.

The lady is quite convinced she *was* Arthur. Furthermore she sees nothing strange or inconsistent in the fact she once was a man. 'Some people come back to this life many times,' she explained, 'and in very different forms... there seem to be no rules, save those of cause and effect.

'Arthur had this great charisma. But he wasn't the chivalrous character that some of the story-tellers would have us believe. As a young man he was keen on women and fathered as many as fifteen children in various parts of Britain by various women.'

In both interviews, she genuinely claimed Arthurian links with the whole of the Westcountry, including Cornwall. So when today we walk or ride across the downs that bear the great King's name, we may truly be following in his famous footsteps.

King Arthur's Hall remains a puzzle.

Fact is nobody knows when these banks were built – or why. They stand alone, rectangular on the skyline, approximately fifty yards along and twenty in width. Today, they are weathered down to the height of a jockey, something like five feet. Today, too, the interior is fractionally lower than the surrounding moorscape, and is partly under water.

Inside King Arthur's Hall, large stones were set up on end as a retaining wall and something like three score are still in position. With the weathering of the bank beyond, they now stand freely, gaunt sculptures, somehow generating the impression you are standing inside some primitive temple – and maybe you are doing just that.

Not even the modern fencing around it can destroy this very primitive quality.

Left: **King Arthur's Hall on a Saturday afternoon in September.**

Blisland

Blisland is unique: the only village in all Cornwall built round a green. Blisland springs a surprise too in that it's not at all characteristic of a Moorland village. In fact, unless you approach it from an easterly direction, you would be forgiven for thinking of it as anything but a village belonging to Bodmin Moor. That village inn, The Royal Oak, and the green, so typical of the English not Cornish countryside, might make you think you have strayed into Devon or another English county – certainly not Cornwall.

Right: **Postman at Blisland 1905.**

Left: **Boys playing cricket on the village green at Blisland.**

Inside Blisland Church. Sir John Betjeman on a
visit here wrote: 'A wonderful inland parish full
of variety. Its glory is its church ...'

Inspiration and Idea

'Q' – Sir Arthur Quiller Couch – in his study on
the eve of his 80th birthday, November 1943.
Note the Q paperweight.

Here on the Moor you understand that the breadth and space are dominant features in many of our Cornish landscapes: pictorial quality, relying on basic elements of water, earth and sky. Landscapes in books are different, more crowded; authors packing paragraphs with incident and movement. But here the painter faces simplicity itself: wide surfaces, large forms. Yet is it so simple – translating the bareness and the beauty on to canvas?

Maybe that is why painters generally have tended to go to the coast and not come here. Maybe that's why there has been no school of Bodmin Moor painters – neither interestingly has there been a Dartmoor school.

In contrast though a number of writers have derived ideas and inspiration from the Moor: Tennyson, Hawker and 'Q', then later Dame Daphne du Maurier, Geoffrey Grigson and James Turner, and, more recently, E. V. Thompson. They have all been fired by the varying moods of this wilderness.

Left: **St Breward Church – surely one of the highest, if not the highest, church in Cornwall.**

Right: **Davidstow airfield, built by the Americans in the last war: a most illogical site, their plans were foiled by thick persistent mist.**

84

Rough Tor and Brown Willy

Rough Tor may be fractionally shorter than Brown Willy, but it has the more interesting summit.

The rock formation is fantastic. A cluster, stacked one upon another, makes you think of some miserly giant, from the long ago, stacking – and counting – his coins. It is a setting which fires the imagination. Here stones, incredibly sculptured by Nature, surround you; some, in the words of Dame Daphne du Maurier, 'shaped like giant furniture, with monstrous chairs and twisted tables'.

Rough Tor – for me – is one of the great grandstands of Cornwall. On a diamond-sharp day it is as if you are perched high above a living map of Cornwall.

Peggy Garside, a neighbour of ours when we lived at Bossiney, had met Alaister Crowley when he came to Cornwall years earlier. 'The wickedest man in the world,' some people called him, but Peggy thought him a 'rather delightful fellow'. She didn't have the slightest interest in the black arts, felt he had only a very tiny following here in Cornwall, but was sure Crowley had used Rough Tor for some rituals.

Peggy Garside only revealed all this after I had had a strange experience on top of Rough Tor.

Back in the 1960s, I was doing a lot of journalism for *The Cornish Magazine*, then edited by John Saxton. It was agreed I should do a feature for the magazine on Rough Tor and Brown Willy. Early one September morning, I set off, accompanied by photographer Bryan Russell and a tan and white terrier called Tex. Tex's presence, in a curious way, did two things: it ruined the expedition and, at the same time, helped to sharpen my probings into Supernatural possibility.

The higher we climbed, that beautiful September morning, the more apprehensive the little dog became – that in itself was strange because he was normally a pugnacious character. Once on top of Rough Tor, Bryan Russell got to work with his cameras, but Tex hid in a crevice.

Brown Willy, on the other side, had a wonderfully beckoning quality, as the haze dissolved, sunlight rimmed the skyline. But Tex refused to go another inch. He shook like a seriously-ill animal, and I became so concerned about his condition, we called off the whole project, deciding to carry Tex back to the car parked down by Rough Tor Farm and drive straight to Mr Byrne, the veterinary surgeon at Camelford. For once, Tex was happy to be carried: a four-legged parcel of agitation. His tremors were so violent I wondered if he was about to die.

Rough Tor: '... for me one of the great grandstands of Cornwall.'

Left: **Painter Felicity Young of Tintagel with her Welsh springer spaniel, Arthur, at work on the Moor. Her paintings often reveal sharp detail, growing from sketches, notes and photographs taken on location.** *Right:* **She captures Brown Willy, seen from Rough Tor.**

90

Half-way down the slope however Tex started struggling. I gently placed him on the ground, and he scampered away; a totally different dog.

Did he detect something beyond our human vision that morning?

I don't know, and frankly have never found anything sinister on my visits to the lovely summit: a place for recharging the batteries in fact.

Curiously though years after that strange September experience author James Turner told me how sentries of the Old Volunteers, encamped nearby, had seen the ghost of Charlotte Dymond, a Cornish girl murdered by her jealous lover one Sunday in 1844.

So hereabouts on the Moor, we are almost certainly on strange Supernatural ground.

But whether you are interested in the Supernatural or not, I still recommend a visit to Rough Tor. From the Camelford side, it is a comfortable walk. Once on this weather-beaten summit stood a chapel dedicated to St Michael. The idea of erecting religious buildings on such high, windswept spots, was due to the old notion that a raging storm was really conflict between the Forces of the Devil and the Heavenly Host – and the comforting belief that sacred buildings, housing holy relics and crosses, kept away the evil spirits.

Maybe that is another reason why Rough Tor *feels* such a good place.

I have sat in the saddle on Brown Willy and watched the different worlds of Cornwall and Devon fade into a morning haze. From the roof of Cornwall, you realise ours is a draughtsman's country. There *is* a sense of geometry in the landscape and you begin to understand the infinite subtleties in the colouring, the greens and the browns, the variations inside just those two shades alone.

Brown Willy is the Cornish Everest. 1,375 feet may be a relatively modest height when we think of the towering giants in other places, but, in this terrain, it assumes the majesty and drama of a mountain. From Brown Willy, deriving from Bryn uhella, meaning highest hill, they say, on a clear morning you can glimpse the Bristol Channel on one side, and the English Channel on the other. That was not my luck. But on that pinnacle I discovered silence is something positive. You can *hear* the silence. Or may be that is delusion, for in such a setting you pick up every hint of sound. The Moors of Cornwall, in mystical fashion, invade all the senses at once; the sheer splendour of the views, the hundred and one lingering smells, the feel of say coarse grass underfoot, the music of the birds, or the wind stirring. The Moor is a magical place; you feel incapable of writing a final full stop. You cannot be dogmatic about it: shades are subtle and various, motives can be vague, strangely unsure like twilight covering a mysterious country – which the Moor often is – or a sleeper waking from deep slumber.

Left: **Rough Tor: '... shaped like giant furniture ...'**

Left: That beautiful Westcountry writer, the late Ronald Duncan, once told me when writing about scenery he felt as though 'ink had turned to treacle'. Twenty years ago, I didn't really understand what the great man was talking about, but now I *know* the dangers: understand that overwriting can turn the landscape more purple than the heather – and this is especially true out on the Moor.

Always perceptive, sometimes caustic, Ronald Duncan once asked probingly: '… how many of us can stand living in a wilderness without becoming oppressed by its loneliness? Although we have laid all the phantoms of headless horses and baying hounds which used to haunt Yes Tor and Brown Willy, why do we still flee… Is it that we are running from ourselves, the ghosts that we've become?'

It's an uncomfortable thought, and again may be the Moor speaks to us, challenges us – so that we begin to see our real selves.

ACKNOWLEDGMENTS:

Most writers – truthful ones at least – usually owe a debt to others. I am especially indebted to three people who have done the vast majority of photographs and drawings for this journey: photographers Ray Bishop and Marylou North and painter Felicity Young. Nearly all their work has been especially commissioned for *The Moors of Cornwall*.

I must also thank the people who talked to me or gave me permission to quote from their work. They have all had something special to say about the magic of our Cornish Moors. Thanks also to Linda Turner who has typed the manuscript, and Brenda Duxbury and Angela Thomas for their thoughtful editing and proof reading.

Land's End
St Teath, Bodmin, Cornwall

Also available

UNKNOWN CORNWALL
by Michael Williams
84 drawings and photographs nearly all especially commissioned for this publication, portraying features of Cornwall rarely seen on the published page.
'... a treasure chest of rich jewels that will surprise many people who pride themselves on a thorough knowledge ...'
Western Evening Herald

100 YEARS ON BODMIN MOOR
by E. V. Thompson. 145 photographs.
A rich harvest of old photographs and picture postcards, reflecting life on the Moor for a century with perceptive text.
'... will entice the present day visitor to Cornwall to explore the Moor ...'
Pamela Luke, The Methodist Recorder

PEOPLE AND PLACES IN CORNWALL
by Michael Williams
Featuring Sir John Betjeman, Marika Hanbury Tenison, Barbara Hepworth and seven other characters, all of whom contributed richly to the Cornish scene.
'... outlines ten notable characters ... whose lives and work have been influenced by ''Cornwall's genius to fire creativity''... a fascinating study.'
The Cornish Guardian

SEA STORIES OF CORNWALL
by Ken Duxbury. 48 photographs.
'This is a tapestry of true tales', writes the author, 'by no means all of them disasters – which portray something of the spirit, the humour, the tragedy, and the enchantment, that is the lot of we who know the sea.'
'Ken is a sailor, and these stories are written with a close understanding and feel for the incidents.'
James Mildren, The Western Morning News

MYSTERIES IN THE DEVON LANDSCAPE
by Hilary Wreford & Michael Williams
Outstanding photographs and illuminating text about eerie aspects of Devon. Seen on TSW and Channel 4. Author interviews on DevonAir and BBC Radio Devon.
'... reveals that Devon has more than its share of legends and deep folklore.'
Derek Henderson,
North Devon Journal Herald

PEOPLE & PLACES IN DEVON
by Monica Wyatt
Dame Agatha Christie, Sir Francis Chichester, Dr David Owen, Prince Charles and others. Monica Wyatt writes about eleven famous people who have contributed richly to the Devon scene.
'A very interesting title from this rapidly expanding publishing house. Indeed, for a ''cottage'' industry it's going from strength to strength, it's territory now covering an area from Bristol to Land's End.'
Irene Roberts, The South Hams
Newspapers

DARTMOOR IN THE OLD DAYS
by James Mildren. 145 photographs.
James Mildren is an author who is at home in the wilderness of his Dartmoor.
'Lovers of Dartmoor will need no persuasion to obtain a copy. To anybody else, I suggest they give it a try. It may lead to a better understanding of why many people want Dartmoor to remain a wonderful wilderness.'
Keith Whitford, The Western

SEA STORIES OF DEVON
In this companion volume to Sea Stories of Cornwall nine Westcountry authors recall stirring events and people from Devon's sea past. Well illustrated with old and new photographs, it is introduced by best-selling novelist E. V. Thompson.
'The tales themselves are interesting and varied but the real strength of the book lies in the wealth of illustration, with photographs and pictures on practically every page.'
Jane Leigh, Express & Echo

NORTH CORNWALL IN THE OLD DAYS
by Joan Rendell. 147 old photographs.
These pictures and Joan Rendell's perceptive text combine to give us many facets of a nostalgic way of North Cornish life, stretching from Newquay to the Cornwall/Devon border.
'This remarkable collection of pictures is a testimony to a people, a brave and uncomplaining race.'
Pamela Leeds, The Western Evening Herald

THE CORNISH COUNTRYSIDE
by Sarah Foot. 130 illustrations, 40 in colour.
Here, in Bossiney's first colour publication, Sarah Foot explores inland Cornwall, the moors and the valleys, and meets those who work on the land.
'Sarah Foot sets out to share her obvious passion for Cornwall and to describe its enigmas... It is a book for those who are already in love with Cornwall and for those who would like to know her better.'
Alison Foster, The Cornish Times

VIEWS OF OLD CORNWALL
by Sarah Foot.
Nearly 200 old picture postcards from the Peter Dryden collection, with text by Sarah Foot, all combine to recall Cornwall as she once was.
'... will be certain to start the talk flowing of days gone by.'
The Cornishman

RIVERS OF CORNWALL
by Sarah Foot. 130 photographs, 45 in colour.
The author explores six great Cornish rivers: the Helford, the Fal, the Fowey, the Camel, the Lynher and the Tamar.
'... full of beautiful colour and black and white photographs with a friendly and succint text from the pen of the well-known author.'
The Cornish Banner

DISCOVERING BODMIN MOOR
by E. V. Thompson. 45 photographs and map.
E. V. Thompson, author of the bestselling novel, *Chase the Wind,* set on the eastern slopes of Bodmin Moor, explores the Moor past and present.
'... shows the moor in all its aspects – beautiful, harsh, romantic and almost cruel... how well he knows the character of the moor.'
The Editor, Cornish Guardian

CURIOSITIES OF SOMERSET
by Lornie Leete-Hodge
A look at some of the unusual and sometimes strange aspects of Somerset.
'Words and pictures combine to capture that unique quality that is Somerset.'
Western Gazette

GHOSTS OF SOMERSET
by Peter Underwood
The President of the Ghost Club completes a hat-trick of hauntings for Bossiney.
'... many spirits that have sent shivers down the spines over the years ...'
Somerset County Gazette

UNKNOWN BRISTOL
by Rosemary Clinch
Introduced by David Foot, this is Bossiney's first Bristol title. 'Rosemary Clinch relishes looking round the corners and under the pavement stones ...'
'... covers many of lesser known aspects of the city and its people.'
Pulmans Weekly News

EXMOOR IN THE OLD DAYS
by Rosemary Anne Lauder. 147 photographs.
The author perceptively shows that Exmoor is not only the most beautiful of our Westcountry moors but is also rich in history and character: a world of its own in fact.
'... contains scores of old photographs and picture postcards... will provide a passport for many trips down memory lane ...'
Bideford Gazette

WESTCOUNTRY MYSTERIES
Introduced by Colin Wilson
A team of authors probe mysterious happenings in Somerset, Devon and Cornwall. Drawings and photographs all add to the mysterious content.
'... strange goings-on in Britain's south-west peninsula... recommended.'
Doc Shiels, Fortean Times

HEALING, HARMONY & HEALTH
by Barney Camfield
Healing in its various forms, the significance of handwriting and dreams, and psycho-expansion.
'If you are tuned in to the right wave length of new age thinking... you won't want to put it down until you get to the last page.'
David Rose, Western Evening Herald

UNKNOWN DEVON
by Rosemary Anne Lauder, Monica Wyatt and Michael Williams. 73 illustrations.
In Unknown Devon three writers explore off-the-beaten track places in Devon.
'If you want to extend your knowledge of hidden Devon then this well-illustrated book is a handy companion.'
Mid-Devon Advertiser

We shall be pleased to send you our catalogue giving full details of our growing list of titles for Devon, Cornwall and Somerset and forthcoming publications.

If you have difficulty in obtaining our titles, write direct to Bossiney Books, Land's End, St Teath, Bodmin, Cornwall.